PASSIVE INCOME STRATEGIES:

A manual with many ideas to start and know the best stream of income. The Beginners Guide to investing for conquer freedom with online business system.

Table of Contents

Introduction

Passive income is not a get rich quick scheme as statistics have shown that most working people rely on their active incomes. That can be wrong because anything can happen, and they lose their jobs. That would mean that they won't have anything to fall back on which is very dangerous. One should strive to have most of their income passively maybe at least 95%. Passive income is not just for the rich but for anyone that is willing to learn and try new things. Be a little adventurous with your money and time to make a little extra money.

Hard work is very valuable for people that want to make a living with passive income. Some people have been able to retire early because they have made enough money and keep making it as they travel the world. This is because they realize that one must work harder at the beginning so that money can keep flowing later. They do their homework first so that they can enjoy later. Remember that passive income requires patience before you see a return on your investment; therefore, don't give up even when it takes longer than other people. Your journey is different, and maybe you may have to change your method a little bit.

It is important to connect with people as you start this journey. You may need mentors that will show you the ropes of the industry. Take notes and learn from them. You will need a community of people that work in the same industry so that you can exchange notes and help each other when you are stuck. You also need to create a tribe of people that believe in you and will support your venture financially. These are the most important because they are the reason you will keep thriving. They will buy and recommend their friends to buy. These are the people you must keep happy and engaged at all times. You should genuinely care about them and give them what they want at all times.

There are many more ways to make passive income than I could fit on this single volume. Keep learning about more ways, and even if you pick one of the ways I have shown you, you can keep improving on till you become a true master that other people can study. Don't be selfish. If you are good at a method of passive income, there are people somewhere that are struggling that could need your help. Offer courses to earn more passive income or offer free training as your way to give back to others.

Chapter 1. Features of passive income

Less reliance on a nine-to-five job.

More freedom to manage your time

The opportunity to develop new ideas and sources of making money

Full control of your income level

Control of your destiny

Why you should consider passive income today

I don't just want to tell you about passive income ideas in this book as it's way too easy to stop just at that. I also want you to take proactive measures in building wealth for yourself and putting an end to financial stress by showing you the clear reasons why you should consider passive income ideas. Once you internalize these reasons you will not want to go back to the old ways.

Beyond the fantastic feeling of receiving regular cash deposits without active work, passive income provides great benefits that will make you consider it an indispensable tool for creating wealth and gaining financial freedom.

1.   Improved Financial Security

Despite how great your yearly job performance assessments may usually be, it can be difficult to know exactly what's going to happen at your day job. Maybe your organization hits a rough patch and the company needs to downsize. Maybe they can't give you a long-expected raise or they need to cut your benefits package. Maybe your boss had a bad day and your evaluation wasn't as stellar as it typically is. All of these situations are not something that has to do with how well you do your job which is actually the only thing you do have control over at your job. Unfortunately, your employer has full control of all such situations. Passive income helps put you in control so that you can be the one calling the shots.

Developing different methods of passive income helps diversify your cash streams as having only one stream of income these days is one of the riskiest strategies you can rely on. It creates assets you can easily control. The more passive income you have coming in, the safer you'll feel in case something does happen at your regular job. The same way you don't invest all your money in just one stock, you also shouldn't depend on earnings from one place alone. The principles are the same even though the situations are different.

2.   Freedom to manage your own time

Passive income greatly increases the amount of time in the day for you. I quickly realized that people working standard jobs can't be happy with the amount of free time they have and with money which they are earning. Instead of being bound by the eight-hour, Monday-Friday workday, you can retain that job while also benefitting from the added advantages and money generated by your passive income ideas. The other option that will also be open to you is to work a part time job instead which will probably end up being more fun than the usual corporate grind. You can also rely on your passive income entirely if you feel that you reached that level. Furthermore, if you have disciplined spending habits, passive income allows you to save up, giving you even more financial freedom. Financial intelligence is way beyond the scope of this book, but all that I will say on that topic is that nothing you can buy with money will make you as happy as financial freedom. Put the money from your passive income ideas as investments into new methods of generating and watch your active workforce of dollars grow!

3.   A sure road to financial freedom

If you bought a ticket that made you into a lottery winner this weekend, would you plan to go to work at the beginning of the week? Is your job your calling or just a way to pay the bills? A lot of people would be happy to have more time to do everything they would like to do, rather than spending all our time working to fulfill other people's dreams. Individuals who take passive income seriously can be rewarded with that freedom.

You will need to patiently build your passive income streams before you can say goodbye to your job. Everyone wants the magic key to immediate escape, but that commitment is important. Important thing is to know the fundamentals so that you can take action and learn from mistakes. Waiting for the magic pill or some missing strategy is the easiest way to waste time. You are not forced to stay at job after you have more than enough passive income for your expenses and at that point, you can leave whenever you want. True success isn't really about the money, it's about the freedom.

Chapter 2. Affiliate Marketing

If you are looking to generate some extra income in the short-term to make it possible for you to invest in a more lucrative option in the long-term then affiliate marketing is likely a good choice. Affiliate marketing is one of the most common entry points for many people into the world of running a passive income business online and it is easy to see why. It really is that simple, all you need to do is find a product you like, talk about why you like it in a way that is compelling for others and then give your viewers an easy way to purchase the product you like for themselves. As such, it is also a common entry point for those who are looking to generate a passive income stream as well.

When it comes to successfully marketing affiliated products, there are two sides to the equation with the creator or primary distributor of the product on one side and you, as the affiliate marketer, on the other. With this in mind, it is easy to see affiliate marketing as spreading the benefits of product creation as well as the marketing of products across a range of different group where each group receives a slice of one whole financial pie according to their individual contributions.

Generally speaking, the person on the other side of the equation from you, as the affiliate marketer, is going to be the merchant, which means they will be relying on you and people like you to get their products out there to the public. This type of marketing can take a wide variety of different forms, though the most common of which is by simply reviewing products that are targeted at specific niches or groups. The target for these informational advertisements is the buying audience which is the specific portion of the general audience that the merchant is targeting. As an affiliate marketer, your job is to target the buying audience as specifically and effectively as possible.

Types of compensation: There are several different compensation models that merchants and publishers can agree to, each works differently which means they all have very different earnings potential. While certain types of compensation models are a natural fit for certain products, it is important to keep in mind that a large part of ensuring a reliable amount of compensation is choosing products that you can reliably convince others to buy.

If you sign up to market products via the pay per lead model, then you won't actually be selling anything directly. Rather, you will be working to convince users to provide their details to a specific database that will be used to advertise to them at a point and time in the future. Before you sign up for this type of program it is important you understand exactly what you will be asking of people and what the compensation is going to be.

Generally, you can expect between $2 and $20 for each lead that is generated based on the amount of information you get the future customer to provide. This type of affiliate marketing agreement is typically found with service providers of varying types including internet service providers and smartphone companies. This is typically thought of as one of the most difficult affiliate marketing programs due to the internet's natural distaste for giving up private information. As such, it is best undertaken by those who have already built an online following of individuals who implicitly trust them completely.

Pay per sale affiliate marketing is the most common type available and is offered through Amazon.com on practically any item you are interested in shilling for.

To start, you simply sign up with Amazon as an affiliate and you are then provided unique links to the items you request. Then, for every time an item is sold through your link, you receive a small percentage of the profits.

The pay per click model doesn't require you to actively strive to sell products, it simply requires that you have a website that is visited regularly. You then sell ad space on your site and are paid a few cents every time someone clicks on one of the ads regardless of whether or not a sale is then generated. The starting rate for this type of affiliate marketing is typically just 1 or 2 cents per click but if you build your website into something that gets thousands of visits each day then the payout can increase substantially.

Costs: To find the best success in the tides of affiliate marketing, your best bet is to get yourself set up with a website:

- Domain name

- Hosting

- SEO and keyword tools

- PPC

- Email Marketing

- Outsourcing

- Images

If you are paying for just the basic costs of starting a website, you will be paying only around $10 each month, which is just $120 per year to start your own side business. Not bad, right? To give your website real potential, however, you need to ensure you are utilizing the right marketing tools.

Nevertheless, there is more to consider than just the costs, if you wish to truly succeed in affiliate marketing, you will have to learn and become a bit of an expert in a number of areas. When you become a marketer, you are left to be the problem-solver as well as the decision-maker. There is no one guidebook to reference to, and with competitors being the only folks that can aid you, you don't want to reveal your campaign information.

When it comes to making adequate decisions, many internet marketers learn the value of following their gut. Studying psychology, using decision matrices and logic trees, and developing strategies to make better choices will help you to become an expert in the craft of marketing online.

Choosing a niche: A niche market is a small and specialized chunk of a larger, more general market which in turn comes with a specific selection of product interests and customer demographics. To illustrate, consider the market for online dating which can then further be broken down into things such as sacred sexuality, green dating, polyamory, soulmates and more and each of these can then be further broken down into sub categories such as soulmates over the age of 40 and gay green dating. In a world where every niche is already accounted for, sub niches are a great place to start, though not every sub niche is automatically going to be profitable which is where doing the right research comes into play.

When it comes to starting down the path to affiliate marketing, it is important to approach the process with the idea of forming a brand around the thoughts and opinions you currently hold or are interested in learning more about. Once upon a time, you could have a site that functioned purely as an aggregate of a specific affiliate marketer's products but any more, that type of site will be removed from Google search results as it does little to add new value to the Internet. This means that you will need to be marketing yourself as much as the products in question when it comes to finding success in the pay per sale or pay per lead world.

Generating content

Facebook: If you wish to promote affiliate products on Facebook, the best way to do so is by using Facebook's built in advertising options. Creating targeted Facebook advertisements is a great way to ensure that the people you are targeting are specifically interested in a specific hobby or interest. With their extreme access to data, studies show that Facebook targeting is up to 90 percent more accurate than its competitors.

To create an ad that you want to run on Facebook, you simply use the Facebook

Ads Manager which can be accessed at Facebook.com/Business. After ensuring your Ads Manager account is linked to your regular account you will want to create an ad campaign and start by choosing a goal for the advertisement in question. Advertising goals range in specificity but, in general, you are likely going to want to choose increase conversions on a website or send viewers to a website, though other options may apply.

YouTube: Unlike in other marketing avenues, the genre of video product reviews is healthy enough to not need to be couched in any other type of content. In fact, short and to the point videos expressing the strengths and weaknesses of various products routinely rack up a million or more views when done properly. From there it is simply a matter of setting up a traditional affiliate program and putting a link to the item in question in your descriptions.

Creating a YouTube account is as easy as having a Google Account and going to YouTube.com to claim your page. From there it is important to post new content frequently so that you can build up an audience who expects new videos related to your niche. Think 3 or 4 a week to start, as you want as many people to subscribe as possible.

When it comes to creating product review videos the first thing you will want to keep in mind is that they should always be less than 3 minutes in length. A majority of the interest in these videos comes from individuals who are looking for help making a buying decision in the moment.

Content people want

Detailed product reviews: A review of a product will naturally slip past the standard defenses that many people put up towards sales pitches while still containing virtually all of the same information of a good pitch without any of the traditional stigma that typically comes along with the process. Remember, a review can help customers avoid wasting their money on a shoddy product while a sales page is considered an especially pushy advertisement.

The easiest way to go about doing product reviews is to focus on a single product or group of products with an exceptionally critical eye. This means you are going to want to single out the various weaknesses of the product or product line as well as focusing on its strengths and what makes it unique. It is important to keep in mind that this type of content needs to come off as unbiased as possible otherwise the illusion will be ruined. This means it is important to intersperse positive reviews with negative ones to allow your target audience to come to the right conclusions about your review integrity. When writing these reviews feel free to include two or three links where the reader can purchase the product if they are so inclined.

Consider niche questions: Regardless of the niche you occupy, you are going to likely be familiar with dozens of commonly asked questions regarding various aspects of the niche or the portion of it you occupy, if not both. You can start off by answering these in a fashion that is as in-depth as you feel that each warrant. Once you post a few of these types of pieces you will likely notice an uptick in emails from users with questions of your own. Not only is this a great way to get in touch with your users directly, it is an evergreen fount of topics for future blogs as well. Not only will this type of content help with current customer retention, it will also likely bring in a fair amount of new traffic as well. In fact, as much as 70 percent of all of Google's traffic stems from people asking the types of questions you should be answering.

To create this type of content, the first place you are going to want to look is to the products and services that you are already marketing. If you don't find that you can produce enough questions to fill a blog post off the top of your head, then heading to Google and poking around in your niche is a good place to start.

Chapter 3. Amazon KDP (Kindle Direct Publishing)

Are you a creative person who wants to make money in the next 24 hours? Then you might be interested in finding out more details about Amazon Kindle Direct Publishing. Just think about it! Not all writers may have the skills of George R.R. Martin or Dan Brown and finding a publisher and an agent to best look after his/her interests may not be something that the writer can afford. But don't let this discourage you, as there are other options to make money from writing and selling books, (eBooks in this case). Amazon, the largest online retailer in the US and also the provider of the biggest marketplace, can offer you this opportunity. It also has its benefits, as you can see below:

• Compared to agents and publishers, Amazon can let you keep a lot more of your money;

• With over 90 million Prime members in the US alone, and more than 300 million customers worldwide, you can reach a vast audience;

- There are no fees involved for the self-publishing service on Amazon KDP, as it's absolutely free.

Theoretically, anyone can publish a book (or several books) on Amazon, but before you get your hopes up, you need to make sure that your book will become an absolute success. As Amazon includes the biggest library on the planet, with so many books, you will need to make sure that your book will stand out from the crowd. That is, you will need to come up with a strategy in order to become a successful writer on this platform. This chapter will provide you valuable information about how to validate your book idea, how to package your book to look like a bestseller, create a pre-launch plan, a step-by-step guide on how to launch your book, but also how to keep the sales going and money coming.

Let's start with the beginning, as before you start writing your first words on your eBook, you will need to make sure that your book idea will be catchy to the wide audience. It's a pity to waste time on an eBook that no one will read it. At this point, the right thing to do is to look at the competition and find out answers to the following questions:

• Can you find similar books? If you simply can't find any title related to the one you are thinking of, this can mean this is not a popular topic, so it's not a good idea to publish such a book, as nobody can be that original;

• Are you prepared to compete? Checking your competition can help you understand better how well your book could perform if it sells like hotcakes, or it doesn't sell at all (or in only a few copies);

• Do you think there are enough buyers? One thing to make sure in this case is that you will have an interested audience for your book, so people who want to buy your book

The following steps can help you find the answers to your questions.

Step 1) Find your category on Amazon. Just go to amazon.com, in the "Departments" section, and then select the "Kindle E-Readers & Books" section, followed by the "Kindle Books" option. To find the most popular categories, simply select "Best Sellers & More" and then "Kindle Best Sellers". In the next menu, please select Kindle eBooks and pick the category and subcategory which is closest to your idea. After selecting the subcategory, you should start investigating your potential competitors.

Step 2) Make sure you check the Top 20 Books for the category you selected. Of course, you will probably not have the exact title with the competing books, but you may need to look over books with similar topics and themes. Therefore, after going through the first 2 steps, you have answered the first question for yourself. The next steps should provide you answers for the other questions as well.

Step 3) Look for the Best Seller Rank for the top books in your category. The best way to find out whether you can compete or not in a category, and if there are enough buyers, you will need to find out how well the books from the category sell. Amazon will not give you the option to find the updated sales numbers, but if you check the "Best Seller" rank you should be able to find a rough estimate. Therefore, in the Product Details section of a book, you can discover this information. Higher ranks will mean automatically more copies sold, so that's a competitor that's very hard to beat. Therefore, the ideal situation for you will be an average rank, so not too low or too high.

- Rankings above 1,000 can be very competitive writers and a great number of sales

- If the rankings are between 1,000 and 30,000, the writers are less competitive, but there are still good sales numbers

- Any rankings below 30,000 mean less competitive writers and very poor sales numbers

Obviously, the middle rankings are where you will need to place yourself, as the category is not too competitive and the sales are decent enough. You will need to target the categories where you think you can come in the top 3 books. If you manage to do so, there will be a good chance that your book will be listed in the "Hot New Releases" section, so your sales will go through the roof. If your book comes up high enough in that list, your book will benefit from a lot of exposure. When readers are going through categories, they are not going through all the pages, so there are lower chances for your book to be seen if it's listed on the 3rd or 4th page, or beyond that. This is why you need to rank higher in the category, so choosing the right category is highly important.

How to Present your Book as a Bestseller?

People always say "don't judge a book by its cover," well the cover is the thing that catches the eye of the reader in the first, so at least when it comes to selling eBooks on Amazon, this saying doesn't apply at all. In this section, you will find out how you can cover some important parts of your book, like the cover design, the title, the book description, and the formatting.

Step 1) Create a catchy, descriptive and memorable book title. Keep in mind that the title of your book can be the most important marketing decision when it comes to your book. Therefore, a good title may get the attention of readers, so your book might have a chance of becoming successful, but a bad title will guarantee the failure of your book. You need to get it right when it comes to the title, so make sure you think through properly the main components of your title: the title itself and the subtitle. Try to come up with something catchy, memorable, as it hints at the topic of your book and should have great success with your audience. The subtitle should be different and longer than the main title, as it should clarify what the book is about. Therefore, you will need to ask yourself the following:

1) Can the book solve any of the reader's problems?

2) Are there any positive outcomes provided by the book?

3) How can the book influence your readers? Can it make a difference for them?

In order to find the title that best suits you, you will need to check plenty of other titles and subtitles. This is how you write down your favorites for both the main title part, but also the subtitle part. If you have found some interesting titles, then you will need to adjust them properly to suit your needs. You can use also some sensory words that can appeal to the readers' sense of smell, taste, touch, sound or sight.

Step 2) Get a cover that catches the eye of others. When you meet a person for the first time, you know the importance of the first impression. Well, the cover is a part of the first impression that readers form about your book. So make sure you use the proper tools to make it very appealing, as a sloppy and cheap cover will not get you too many readers. Therefore, the proper cover should have the following characteristics:

• a very clear and legible title. The title should easily be readable, even when the eBook is shown in the size of a thumbnail. If readers can clearly see your title, they will click on it, if not, they will just ignore that thumbnail. This is why you will need to avoid small and hard to read fonts;

• an outstanding design. Using a skilled graphic designer can make a huge difference, as you will need exceptional graphics on the cover to catch the eye of readers. Don't try to design the cover yourself, unless you are a skilled graphic designer. You will need to spend some money on these kinds of services, so don't cheap out, as a well-made cover will recover the costs you paid for graphic design. You can also try Fiverr, to find professional designer's samples.

Step 3) Make sure the book is pretty on the inside. This is all about properly formatting your eBook, so you will need to save your file in a file type that is Kindle-friendly like .epub or .mobi. You can take care of this task, or you can hire a professional, it's your call. Some writers can use some specialized software for formatting like Vellum, but this software is only compatible with Mac. If you use a Windows operating system, you can try Book Design Templates or Reedsy. You can also try to do it manually if you are tech-savvy enough, but if you are not, you might want to consider hiring someone to do it for you. There are plenty of freelancers out there who can help you with this task in exchange of a decent fee. After you format the book, don't forget to proofread it using a Kindle or the Kindle app.

Step 4) Come up with a description that can sell the book for you. Your title and cover may be the first things to lure readers to your book, on the Amazon sales page, but a proper book description will definitely awaken their interest and can influence them to buy the book. Before buying anything, readers would like to know what the book contains and how they can benefit from it. If your description is not well-written, then readers will not hit the buy button. This is why the book description should not be treated as a summary of the book, it should be like a sales letter, encouraging people to read the book and also providing some reasons to do so. So don't briefly mention the content of your book, persuade the reader to buy it! Focus on some main points of the book, list some benefits for reading it (use bullet points), describe why the reader should buy the book.

The Pre-Launch plan includes a few things to do before launching your book:

Step 1) Create your team of reviewers. As you probably already know, Amazon is a review-based environment, so without reviews, readers will not be able to easily find your book. There's nothing more valuable on the Amazon platform than getting reviews, so a new book might experience difficulties in order to be sold. However, it doesn't have to be like this. You can save yourself from struggling to sell at the beginning, by simply assembling your own team of reviewers. Get some people to review the book before its launch and promote the reviews during your launch week. This is why it's important to build your own network of authors and bloggers, as if you get influencers to review your book, this will be valuable in the eyes of the readers. You will need to spread the word and reach out to the people in your network, but make sure you explain to them what's expected of them.

• Explain to them they are reading an advanced reader copy of your book and you need a review from them to be posted during the first week of the launch

• You can also encourage them to share the book on social media or in their email list. Of course, this is optional, but it will mean a lot to you.

If you only want to get a certain number of reviews, make sure you ask twice the number of people to review it, because probably only half of them will review it. For your launch, you will need to a minimum of 25 reviews, so you will need to reach out to 50 people from your network.

Step 2) Create teasers for your book. Once the book is already written and you have a clear idea of the publishing date, you definitely want to tease your subscribers or potential readers to inform them of what it's coming. You will need to build anticipation, so a weekly newsletter can be very helpful for informing people about the new release, and to make them aware that a new book is coming.

Step 3) Carefully plan your launch and prepare promotional materials. Every step you take before the launch has to be properly scheduled, so you have a very clear idea of what to do each day. Once you have planned everything, make sure you prepare everything you need for the launch, preferably in the weeks prior to launching:

• An email sequence to promote the book to subscribers

• Emails sent to your team of reviewers

- Promotional articles to be published prior to the launch

- Social media posts dedicated to promoting your book

If you don't prepare yourself for the launch, you could panic at one point as you don't have the materials for a successful launch. In order to avoid such a scenario, make sure you plan accordingly and also prepare properly for the launch. This step should start 6 weeks before the launch.

How to keep the sales going and money coming?

In order to succeed from a financial point of view, you will need to follow these simple steps:

1) Raise your price once per week (but also inform your subscribers). If you start at $0.99 the launch price, you can add an extra dollar to your price, until it reaches the final value (let's say $4.99). However, you will need to inform your subscribers of this rise in price, so they will not be surprised. This is how they can see that there is a time frame for the discounted price, so

they will need to jump in and seize the opportunity to get your offer.

2) Keep on posting to get people on your list. Every time you post an article, encourage people to subscribe, as this is how you can increase your fan base. You need to make readers understand what the benefits of being your subscribers are, as they can get special offers or other surprises.

3) You can use an Amazon Ad Campaign for Sales using AutoPilot. Try using PPC (pay-per-click) advertising for writers, as this can form of advertising can totally be worth the investment. Be very careful about the keywords you bid on, constantly monitor their performance, to find out on which ones to keep on bidding, and which ones you will need to set aside.

Chapter 4. Joint Venture Partnerships

What are Joint Venture Partnerships?

A joint venture partnership is when two companies come together so that they can use each other's resources, and then they both benefits. For example, a delivery company may hand out coupons from a manufacturer. The manufacturer gets free delivery of advertisements, and the delivery company will be the exclusive partner to the manufacturer. They are combining their resources to reduce costs and accomplish a goal that neither company could very easily accomplish on their own. While this is the legal definition of a joint venture partnership, for our purposes it will be slightly more expensive, including simply working with another party to pool your resources and make investments that neither party could accomplish on their own.

Your first opportunity at a joint venture partnership should be to promote your existing social media accounts. For example, in books one and two you learned how to earn passive income through Instagram and YouTube. Each account builds on the other, with subscribers from your Instagram account boosting your views on YouTube, and vice versa. This is just the tip of account synergy, and you should partner with other YouTube channels and Instagram accounts. There are some ways to do this, from engaging in larger competitions among the subscribers of both channels, as well as pooling resources on Instagram to get the notice of larger brands for product placement. This will merely offer the opportunity for free advertising but does not quite get at the heart of pooling resources for greater investment. To do this, you will need to partner with a close friend or family member and discuss possible ventures that you can both engage in together, but you would not be able to tackle alone.

In a joint venture partnership, you are not just pooling your monetary resources, but are also your labor. In the ventures for passive income listed below, keep this mind, both for your ability to participate in each venture, but also for the person that you will be working with. You need to trust your partner both regarding their financial commitment, but also their ability to provide labor for any single project. You might be able to gain the financial investment from a partner but find that they are unwilling to put in the labor. To avoid this, it is best to work with someone you know.

Do note that for most joint venture partnerships you have the opportunity to enter a legal agreement. I suggest that you do not do this. Regarding co-promote for your online ventures, this is simply unnecessary, as the income streams will be separate, and your partner will not be able to take over your account and lock you out. Regarding financial investment, a legal agreement might be necessary if you are partnering with someone that you do not know, but note that this adds quite greatly to the cost of starting a venture. You will have to hire a lawyer to write out the agreement, and theoretically, your partner will also have their lawyer review it. It adds a complication that isn't necessary if you are partnering with someone you know. If you were engaging in ventures involving the stock market, this is a case where I would advise a legal agreement. The projects here are cases where it is quite easy to note that both parties are putting up equal investment, and both are splitting the revenue equally. It is harder to make these determinations when dealing with online income.

YouTube, Instagram, and eBook Promotion

The simplest form of a joint venture partnership is the promotion. If you already have made investments in YouTube, Instagram, and eBook writing, you will want to reach out to other entrepreneurs and to try and promote each other. This is more easily done with YouTube and Instagram, as I have not been very successful with promoting eBooks. You should find channels and accounts that are similar to yours since the user base is likely to be interested in both your material and your partner's. You will want to focus on channels and accounts that are similar in size to your own. You must make it clear that you both stand to gain subscribers and is by working together, and that you are not trying to leech their audience, something that could come to mind if your partner is more popular than yourself. This is true if you receive the offer to partner with a channel or account as well– make sure that they are about as popular as you, otherwise you are essentially offering a free promotion with very little in return. The audience size of your partner needs to be worth working together.

Chapter 5. Merch by Amazon

Another Amazon feature that will help you produce passive income is the Merch system. Merch by Amazon allows you to upload styles to be published on t-shirts and offered in the world's largest online marketplace. Amazon provides a print-on-demand assistance and order fulfillment, so you don't have to worry about creating the t-shirts, obtaining a person base, storing stock, shipping, returns, etc. They also handle all the customer service aspects. They don't even ask you for anything to sell on their platform- they just charge costs and charges on your own actual sales.

If you're no artist or designer even, you can make a profit from this ongoing service, but because of the service's popularity, Amazon has made it a bit harder to become a Merch creator. Amazon offers quality requirements to meet up and a 100% fulfillment guarantee for his or her customers, so they would like to make certain the social people offering shirts on their site are worthwhile. There's a waiting list to become among their designers, and you ought to request your invitation to use as soon as you read this and that means you don't miss your opportunity to make passive income with this service.

To be remembered as a creator, you need to request an invitation in order to apply. You'll receive your invitation when Amazon provides space for new content creators, but remember that this wait can be anywhere from a couple weeks to a year.

Once you obtain your invitation, you'll fill out your application. It starts with your business get in touch with information, your social security number, as well as your bank information and routing numbers. In case you are selling shirts as yourself, not as a company, just use your own name and address. In the request type, there is a box for "more information." This package can be extremely helpful in increasing your chance of acceptance. Make hyperlinks to your style portfolio or the look portfolio of your contracted graphic designer, as well as any kind of other sites where you sell products.

If you're not going to personally design your t-shirts, tell them that. Let them know you want to outsource high-quality designs, and link the website of whatever developer you have. Suggest to them that you are a reliable business. In the web site box, link your personal or company site, or your blog.

Once you're accepted to sell your designs, you'll have to come up with good content people would want to purchase. Keep an optical attention out in public areas for what t-shirt designs you see people wearing on the streets, what keywords frequently are being used, and what phrases or image styles are being sold on t-shirts to get. Be sure to match trends on social press also, particularly Twitter, so that you can be among the first to release trend-related or meme-related content when the opportunity arises. Creating trend-related t-shirts can be strike and miss because if the demand for products exists, many creators will be releasing competing items then. But if you will be ahead of the development by being one of the first release a your products, then you can profit greatly.

You can also do key word research by looking through Amazon's Best Sellers and finding which niches appear profitable. This method follows the same manner you'd search profitable niches of eBooks, except it requires into consideration a wider spectrum of products. Using an incognito home window in your browser, head to Amazon's website and search for the most rewarding keywords in your market. Focus on the autocomplete feature and observe what other keywords customers are employing. The reason for using an incognito window is because in any other case Amazon will monitor your searches and this will alter the autocomplete outcomes. This can help you pick a profitable niche.

A few of the niches and sub-niches that are generally going to sell good are niches that people are passionate about. Types of these will be CrossFit sports athletes, vegans, social justice actions, etc. These public people want to represent their beliefs and passions publicly, so a t-shirt that suits them would sell well. When you design your t-shirt, you'll want to make sure your styles are unique and not simply copies of other styles.

Following recent events and social media styles are one method to gain inspiration for profitable merch, but there are always a couple of other ways to make a best-selling design. Evergreen designs are designs that continue steadily to sell again and again, year-round. These designs have become generic usually, but they're reliable for the reason that people will want to buy them always.

Evergreen shirt designs cater to broad niches than more targeted audiences rather. Music, coffee, wine-think about how well-known these topics are on t-shirts in major suppliers. These are examples of evergreen topics you can bottom your designs off of. Holiday designs also sell well. Christmas-themed t-shirts will sell well in the fourth quarter of the year; red and pink romantic relationship themed t-shirts will sell well around Valentine's day, and so on. People prefer to show their holiday celebration and spirit through their clothes.

These three ways are great for reliable profits, nevertheless, you may also make good product sales by creating designs that focus on a specific niche, particularly for underrepresented sub-niches. For example, you could create designs for those who love cats, but a more profitable option may be to design a shirt for owners of hairless cats. Creating a nice design that's very niche can increase your sales.

Generally, the best-selling designs are not overly busy with wild colors and complicated pictures. A simple, text-based style with one very popular keyword may likely sell. Other choices are clever jokes or "inside jokes" inside your niche, logos that are not trademarked, or well-known phrases. Shirts that are designed for fans in a particular sub-market shall also sell, but it is most beneficial to design them in a way that will also be aesthetically satisfying to people beyond that specific group of fans.

Distressed-looking designs sell well but it is important to be sure that the opacity of your image is not too light when getting uploaded or it may not print well. T shirts with high-contrast colours are popular. Colorful styles with lighter colors look extremely pleasing on dark t-shirts, and, on the contrary end of the spectrum, simple designs in dark colors appearance pleasing on lighter t-shirts. In general, in the event that you don't want to make a text-based shirt, then you can certainly also sell well using pictures with active characters, simple designs, and silhouettes. The look area on Amazon's t-shirt template is certainly a rectangular area, but it's recommended in order to avoid creating designs that will print as a rectangular block.

Make sure that you don't make use of any copyrighted components, trademarked images or phrases, or any styles that incorporate someone else's intellectual property. You may use trademark checking websites to make sure your pictures and phrases are not trademarked. Be absolutely sure not to include these components because this will lead to Amazon removing your item and having marks against your account. If your accounts have multiple shirt styles removed from the Amazon marketplace, you will be banned.

Your account may also be suspended if you don't follow Amazon's content guidelines. Your shirt designs might not contain pornography, profanity, intolerant phrases, or references to traumatizing or violent events. Other reasons for suspension could be a shady activity like spending money on product reviews to increase your shirt's Best Retailers rank, creating content material descriptions that don't match your item, linking your personal blog, site, or shop, or offering quicker shipping.

Once you've come up with a couple of design concepts that you think will end up being marketable, you can create the look as a PNG image or hire a freelancer digital media professional do design it for you. Once it's designed, you'll upload it to Amazon. The image should be a PNG file with a 300 dpi (dots-per-inch) resolution and a maximum ration of 15 in. tall by 18 in. long. You'll select a t-shirt template and position your design.

If your design will not take up the whole height of the rectangular area, it is recommended to position the picture higher within the rectangle rather than centered slightly. Once it looks good, choose three colors of shirts which will look good with your style. You can choose more or fewer shades, but three is definitely a strategic number to greatly help your customers with decision making.

Choose what sizes you would like to offer your clothing in, then create a title and explanation. Make sure to make use of multiple high-traffic keywords in your name and write a convincing explanation. Ensure that your description and title are highly relevant to the product's content and so are free of spelling errors. It can be very easy to unintentionally misspell the word "t-shirt" and end up with profanity in your name and description that causes your style to be rejected and your accounts to be at risk, so you'll desire to be extra careful to avoid that.

Once you've uploaded your design and created your item page, it's time to launch and marketplace your shirt. You can advertise your t-shirt by buying and putting on your own design, posting pictures on public media, and posting your design with your friends and family. You can also talk about photos or a link to your style in groups or forums that are linked to your niche, whether these be on Facebook, Pinterest, or various other platforms.

Once you begin making sales, your account will end up being "tiered up. " When you first become an Amazon Merch designer, you can only just upload no more than ten designs. This places you in tier 10. After you've made some sales and Amazon knows you're producing styles that people need it, you'll be upgraded to tier 25. This allows you to market 25 designs at a right time, and so on and so forth.

If you good designs in niches where there is demand upload, Merch by Amazon can be a great opportunity to produce passive income. Plus, you keep the rights to your design, so if you discover that your styles sell well and you'd prefer to create and print your own t-shirts with the same style to market on other platforms you then don't have to worry.

Chapter 6. Airbnb Step-by-Step Process

Now that you have learned about the fundamentals of Airbnb rentals, including how they work and how you can make money from them, it is time to teach you the steps on how to actually engage in this business.

Step 1: Sign up

Airbnb listings are free of charge. You can create as many listings as you want. It is also easy to create these listings. Simply fill out the form with all the necessary information. Your listings would be kept private or hidden until you are ready to have them published.

You can also set a price for different rental duration. For instance, you can set daily, weekly, or monthly rates. You can even charge seasonal rates. This way, you can earn more money if there is a festival or sporting event in your town. You can also make a lot of money during the summer season especially if you live near the beach.

Step 2: Edit your page

Since you are the host, you can set your own house rules. Clearly define what you expect from your guests. Tell them what they are allowed and not allowed to do while on your property.

Use relevant descriptions and attractive photos to advertise your home. You may publish up to twenty-four photos on the site. Whenever a prospective guest becomes interested, he may contact you directly to ask questions.

As the host, you also have the right to accept and turn down booking requests. If you do not like a prospective guest for whatever reason, you are free to turn him down. Just make sure that you either accept or decline the offer in twenty-four hours.

The moment you accepted the reservation, you must coordinate a meeting schedule with the guest. Once his reservation has been completed, you may give a review or feedback. These reviews are great because they help build reference as well as establish a reputation for both the guest and the host.

Step 3: Consider a few crucial factors

See to it that you also consider certain factors before you rent out your property. For instance, you have to consider your location and amenities. If you are in a huge and busy city, you have a good chance of attracting lots of tourists, students on vacation, and businessmen.

New York, Paris, and Los Angeles are examples of cities frequented by tourists and travelers because of their beautiful museums, exciting night life, rich culture, delicious food, and nice tourist spots.

If you live near educational institutions, you can rent out your home to students. These young people want an inexpensive place to live and hang out. Just make sure that you get clear with the house rules so that your home will not be turned into a frat house.

Moreover, you can rent out your property to families or groups of friends who want to hold reunions and other events in your area. You can make a lot of money during peak seasons if you live near the mountains or oceans. These people most likely want to see a great view on their vacation.

You should also consider the amenities available. Is there a nearby bus stop if your home is quite far from the city? Is it possible to reach bookstores, restaurants, parks, and other tourist attractions by walking? Does your home have a parking lot, patio, or garden? Can your guests have their own private kitchen or bathroom if you are only renting out a room?

More importantly, you have to consider the safety and security of your guests as well as their belongings. Make sure that you also provide them with a hotline that they can contact in case of emergencies. For your own security, see to it that you also keep your belongings secured in a closet or room.

Step 4: Create listings

It is very easy to create a listing. In fact, you can finish one in just a couple of minutes. Simply follow the instructions shown on the website. Do not forget to incorporate the following essential elements in your listings to attract the attention of many guests:

a. Intriguing Headline

Nothing keeps a person's attention more than something they find intriguing. Choose a headline that is witty and interesting. It should capture the attention of the reader while giving him enough information at the same time.

Refrain from writing long narratives because they are boring. Keep your headlines brief but detailed. Sum up everything you want to convey in a single line. Remember that the headline is what people see first when they search for Airbnb rentals in your area. So, it has to be enticing.

b. Nice Profile

When you promote your home, you promote yourself as the host as well. Travelers usually go to Airbnb first whenever they want to search for inexpensive accommodations in a particular area. Likewise, they use the site to make immediate personal connections.

So, if you want to capture their attention, your profile should be warm and friendly. Upload a profile picture that makes you appear reliable and personable. Make sure that you also include relevant information to build trust. Your profile should make these prospective guests want to know you better.

c. Accurate Descriptions

It is important to be honest, detailed, and accurate when writing your descriptions about your property.

Some people think that they have to exaggerate and make their homes seem better than they actually are to attract more guests. However, this strategy is not advisable and can backfire massively.

If you lie on your profile, you will be able to attract prospective guests immediately. However, once they find out the truth, they will leave negative reviews and feedback about you on Airbnb. The next time people check out your listings, they would find these bad reviews and get turned off right away.

Obviously, this is not good for your business. So, if you want to make Airbnb rentals work for you, you have to be honest. Do not make any claims or promises that you cannot deliver on as well. For example, if you said that guests can use your Wi-Fi connection, see to it that they actually can. Otherwise, they may file a complaint or even refuse to pay up.

You must also be upfront about what your guests can do on your property. Tell them what they can expect. For example, you can tell them if they can watch cable television, use Wi-Fi, use air conditioning or heater, take a hot shower, use the Jacuzzi or swimming pool, etc.

Tell them how many rooms are in your home and what type of beds you have. Families and groups of friends may prefer double deck beds while couples may prefer a queen-sized bed where they can sleep together.

Make sure that you do not focus on the indoors alone. You must also disclose information about the surroundings. For example, you can reveal to your guests if you live on a busy street.

This way, people who do not want to hear traffic noises or be disturbed by yelling neighbors can avoid renting your home and getting disappointed. On the contrary, young people who prefer urban cities may like your property. They may enjoy its close proximity to bars, restaurants, coffee shops, and dance clubs.

d. Clear Photos

See to it that you take lots of clear photos of your property. Take a picture of every room and area, including your deck, balcony, or yard. This way, the guests can really have a feel of what your home is like.

Use a good camera to produce high quality photos. Take photos from different angles to really showcase your property. Use lighting fixtures if necessary to illuminate dark spots.

If you are not good at taking photos, you can use Airbnb's professional photography services. The company would send professional photographers over to your home to take pictures.

If you live in a good location, Airbnb may even let you avail of their professional photography services for free. You can take advantage of this perk if your photos can help increase the bookings made via Airbnb.

e. House Rules

You can choose from a wide variety of price structures and cancellation policies. You can also set your own house rules. For example, you can say that guests are not allowed to bring other people over or that they are not allowed to smoke.

Step 5: Determine the pricing and timing

Timing is one of the most important aspects of any business. Hence, you must always attempt to schedule an opening at the same time that a major event is happening in your area. This way, you can have more customers or clients.

Take the Super Bowl XLIX as an example. The Airbnb rentals in the Greater Phoenix area greatly profited from this sporting event. Because many people wanted to watch the game, they booked hotel rooms several months in advance. Those who were not prepared had no other choice but to turn to Airbnb rentals.

Last minute clients are actually willing to pay more money. They just want things to be taken care of in the soonest possible time, no matter how much money they have to pay for the services.

Do your best to get positive reviews. Airbnb gives a temporary boost to hosts. Take advantage of this good opportunity.

With regard to pricing, you can check out similar homes or properties to get an idea on how much you can rent out your home. Compare your listing with others so that you can set competitive prices.

If this is your first time to rent out your home, you may offer discounts. This way, you can attract more guests and encourage them to leave positive reviews. Most people like discounts and promos. You can even give your guests freebies or gifts to put them in a good mood.

Guests who were satisfied with your prices and services will most likely leave a positive feedback. So, offering discounted rates at first will not hurt your business. Once you have obtained enough positive reviews, you may raise your prices as well.

You can also find out if your rates are competitive enough by comparing them to the rates of nearby hotels. These places are usually expensive. Take Marriott, for instance. Its rates are at least $169 per night. Guests would have to pay more if they are inviting other people or having a party.

A good rule of thumb is to offer the same price as the hotels in your area. However, instead of merely renting out a room, you can rent out your entire home for this price. This would definitely make guests come to you.

Here are some more tips on how to determine the prices of your Airbnb rentals:

• Know how much your home is worth. What is its value? How much do you pay for mortgage or rent each month? Write down the price that you got and divide it by thirty. Once you get the answer, you can base your rate on this result.

• Study your competition. Observe what they do and how they conduct their business. Your competitors include hostels, hotels, campgrounds, and other Airbnb listings in your area. If you want guests to come to you instead of your competitors, you must be able to offer them better deals. For instance, you can offer a price within the same range as the other listings.

• Offer freebies, add-ons, and other perks. If your house has a washer and dryer, fancy linens, and cable, you can charge additional fees. You can also charge a higher rate than a nearby hotel if you offer a bottle of wine or a fruit basket to guests. You can also charge more if your guests have access to additional garage storage, communal space, or parking space.

• Set a high goal but start low. Since you are new in the industry, you have to set your priorities straight. Focus on attracting guests and obtaining positive reviews instead of beating your competitors. This could mean lowering your prices and giving freebies. Most travelers are in search of the least expensive accommodation. So if you see $100-listings, you may want to offer your place for only $75 per night to attract more views. Over time, you can increase your prices accordingly.

- Be aware of your limitations. Airbnb is basically an ecosystem that governs its own self. The prices of its services are dictated by the supply and demand. You can set your desired price range. However, in order for you to stay competitive on the market, you have to set your price close to what the other hosts offer. If your rate is too high, you will have a hard time attracting guests.

- Take holidays and special events into consideration. You may adjust your rates according to the significance of the event. For example, you can charge higher rates during the Christmas season or whenever there is a festival in your area. Hotels do this all the time. You can use the advanced pricing calendar and pricing tool of Airbnb to help you out.

- Factor in the security deposit. As much as possible, you should ask guests to give you a security deposit that is equivalent to a one night stay at your place. This is for your protection. In case something goes wrong, you can easily recover from the damages because you have funding. This security deposit can cover minor damages, such as scuffed flooring, broken appliances, and damaged furniture.

- Factor in the cleaning fee. Cleaning after guests is not easy, especially if they are a messy bunch. It takes a significant amount of money, energy, and time to complete this task. It does not really matter if you have a cleaning crew or maid to do this. You need to ask your guests to pay for the cleaning fee. This should cover the costs for cleaning bed sheets, mopping, vacuuming, and cleaning the rooms. How much you charge can depend on how big your house is.

- Charge additional fees for additional guests. It is common for guests to hold parties at the house they are staying in. After all, they are on a vacation and they want to have the time of their lives. To protect yourself, you should also charge extra for any additional person staying in your property.

- Charge lower fees for last minute bookings. You may consider dropping your prices if you have unoccupied dates coming up in the next few weeks. Rather than not make any money at all, it is much better to earn a profit from lower rates. You may even receive a positive feedback since guests generally want a good value for their money.

Chapter 7. Blogging

Since it first came about, a lot has evolved about blogging. No longer is it just a personal online diary to record the random musings of the mind. Blogging today has evolved dramatically from a creative outlet for you to pour your thoughts to a passive income medium, and even to a platform where news and information are shared. Even the way blogs look today has changed dramatically from when it first started, with plenty of new marketing and social media features that allow you to share your content quickly and easily. While the essence of blogging continues to remain true to its nature, blogging in today's world needs you to come equipped with a whole host of other skills besides just a flair for writing and some great content to share. If your blog is going to be a sustainable source of passive income long term, you're going to need to do more than just write and click publish. Not only do you have to write in an engaging manner that is coherent and easy to understand by the masses, but you also need to incorporate the use of visuals, PNG files, buttons and social media widgets that make it easy for readers to share your blog across the different social media platforms. There's also something else you're going to need and it's the ability to market your blog professionally. If no one knows your blog is out there, you're not going to get enough traffic to turn your blog into a passive income source.

Here's what you need to do to begin setting up your blog:

- Step 1 - Open an account on your preferred blogging platform. There's an option out there for everyone. WordPress.org, WordPress.com, Wix.com, Blogger, Tumblr, Squarespace, and more.
- Step 2 - Choose the layout you prefer for your blog.
- Step 3 - Customize your blog according to what your needs are and the content you plan to post.
- Step 4 - Write your content, upload visuals, and click publish.

Is Blogging Right for Me?

Blogging can be a great option for anyone who has something to say. If you've got a topic that you're passionate about and you've got a lot of thoughts and ideas on the subject you would like to share, why not use a blog to spread the word. If you're someone who loves information and generally crafting and sharing your opinions, blogging can serve as your creative outlet. Anyone can start a blog, but running and maintaining one is where the real challenge is going to be. A sustainable blog needs to be up to date with fresh ideas and content. Ideally, you want to aim to post something new at least twice a week, so you've always got to have new topics and new ideas on hand.

Blogs are a great way for startup companies to gain visibility among their customers too. Anyone can start a blog of their own: tech companies, hobbyists, crafters, event planners, photographers, bakeries, marketers, and freelancers. The only thing you need to be prepared for is to keep that constant stream of content coming to avoid the risk of being pegged as "inactive" or "outdated' by your readers.

Earning Potential with Blogging
When blogging first got its start, it was all about carving out a name for yourself in the virtual world. These days though, competition is much tougher, and a lot more work is involved before your blog can rise to enough prominence that it lands itself on the first page of Google's search results. The internet today is saturated with blogs covering all kinds of topics and

just about every niche under the sun. Most of today's popular blogging didn't just get there overnight. They've been working on their blog for years before they got to where they are today. Even if you're just starting out now, it's not too late to turn your blog into a potential passive income stream; it's just going to take a little more work to do it.

One thing you should note though is that even if you are working on your blog full time, it is unlikely it's going to be something that can make you rich. It can be turned into a steady income stream, but probably not enough for you to retire in luxury, in case that was what you're hoping for. You're still going to have to complement this with other forms of passive income revenue. To turn your blog into the moneymaker you want it to be, you need great content. Great content is the key to a successful blog; without it, you're going to have nothing more than just another internet platform on your hands. Back in 2012, Blogger.com did some research into this area and discovered that 17% of bloggers were able to turn their blogs into a steady enough revenue for them to support their lifestyle and their family. On the other hand, 81% of bloggers couldn't even make $100 from their blogs.

The amount you stand to make from your blog is going to come down to several factors. Your earning potential is affected by how often you blog, how competitive your topic is, and how effective you are at building a steady audience base that generates the right amount of traffic. This is not going to be an easy process that happens quickly, so you're going to have to be sure this is what you want to do long-term, and you're passionate enough about your blog to keep it running for as long as possible.

Blogging Myths to Overcome

Myths can lead to a lot of misunderstanding and misconception. Even with blogging, and before you begin work on your blog, here are some of the common myths associated with blogging that you want to avoid:

- *Myth: Blogging is A Fad That Won't Last* - Only if you lose interest in your blog. For the bloggers that have turned their site into a steady income stream, it isn't a fad at all. It's their passive income revenue. With even Fortune 500 companies using blogging as a source of reaching out to their target audience, blogging has come a long way and is no longer a short-lived thing anymore. If you're willing to work on it, your blog can turn into a profitable income stream.

- *Myth: Blog Posts Can't Be More Than 500 Words* - Your content should be engaging, regardless of its word count. Whether its 500 words or 1,000 words, if your content is not interesting enough, it's not going to matter because you aren't driving enough traffic. Having in-depth articles that cover topics and subjects your viewers want to read is how you draw them in. It's not about the word count. It's about what you're putting out there. Poorly written content is not going to improve your SEO rankings, so the best thing you can do here is worry a little less about your word count and turn your focus instead towards producing quality content.

- *Myth: You Can't Blog If You Can't Write* - You may not be a first-class writer, but that shouldn't stop you from setting up a blog if you wanted to anyway. Not every reader out there is the same, and some readers actually prefer simpler blogs with less writing and more infographics or visuals instead. Depending on who your target audience is and the kind of content you produce, a blog can still be successful, even without the high-end, college worthy writing skills.

Vlogging

If writing is not really your forte, there's another option you could turn to which has just as much of a chance as becoming a steady passive income stream as blogging does. It's called *vlogging* (video + blogging). That's right, you don't need words all the time to engage with your audience online, not when you've got the option of doing it through videos too. Based on the **EMARKETER'S FINDINGS**, viewers of digital video content have grown exponentially between 2012 and 2016 from 372 million to nearly 700 million. That is an approximate increase of 87%. The time that these viewers spent watching video content has also risen by 120%, with viewers now spending anywhere from 26 minutes to nearly an hour a day watching digital videos online. The growth has mostly been attributed to increasing mobile usage, which has taken over desktop viewing by a mile.

As audiences slowly make the ever-increasing shift towards viewing videos online as a preference, there are certain video content types, which are proving to be more popular and in-demand than others among audiences.

Today, vlogging has emerged as among the most popular forms of digital video content, where video bloggers capture their lives and share their opinions with their audiences through social media platforms. The content of these videos are usually candid, where the vlogger is featured in their videos, which are shot at arm's length, while they record themselves going about their day. These vloggers record themselves throughout the day and share their thoughts on a subject, or report live from a location that they think their fans would be excited about. Content could even include unboxing videos, tutorials, and how-to guides, depending on the subject. Some vloggers even use their space as a place to share their work, performance, music, or any art they have created. Just like blogs, vlogs can encompass any topic of your interest. The only difference between blogs and vlogs is, as the name implies, almost all vlogging content is going to be produced in video format.

Just like blogs, the content of your vlogs needs to look and sound great (since its heavily visual-based), and your page needs to be updated just as regularly so you don't run the risk of losing your followers for not maintaining an active enough presence online.

Is Vlogging Right for Me?

You may know that blogging and writing may not be your strong points, so you're wondering if vlogging is going to perhaps be the better option for you in this case. Vlogging might be a better approach for you if you enjoy any of the following:

- *Speaking on Camera* - You can't be a vlogger if you're shy and self-conscious in front of the camera. The best vloggers out there on YouTube are completely natural, comfortable, and at ease in front of the camera. They make it seem as though they're talking to you directly, instead of through the camera - that's how comfortable they are. Vloggers need to be in front of the camera a lot and you need to imagine your camera is the millions of followers out there who are waiting to hear what you have to say. In fact, to be a successful vlogger, you need to forget about the camera entirely and almost pretend as if it's not there.

- *Spending Time Editing Your Video Content* - This is probably among the more time-consuming aspects of being a vlogger: having to spend hours, sometimes days or weeks, before you've edited your video content until it's ready to be shared with the masses. It's easier today with the availability of the many free video editing tools you can easily find online, along with video tutorials that guide you through the process step-by-step if you've never edited a video before. It's going to be very slow-moving in the beginning and take up a lot of your time, but once you get used to the interface and the features of the software you're using, editing becomes much faster. As you pick up new skills through your multiple editing practice sessions, you'll see the progression of your videos improving in quality. If you don't mind having to spend hours patiently editing your videos before you upload them, go ahead and give vlogging a try.
- *Sharing Your Thoughts with the Public* - You need to be comfortable with the fact that not everyone is going to agree or support your opinion and be okay with that. Successful vloggers understand this, and they're comfortable enough not to let

the occasional negative feedback affect them too much. Not all your viewers are always going to appreciate your suggestions and tips, and some audiences are not going to be gracious with their remarks, either. If you're okay dealing with negative feedback and critics every now and then, you're going to do fine as a vlogger.

- *Continuously Learning* - With the way the digital space continues to evolve these days, there's always going to be a new skill or technique to be learned. Before you begin a vlogging channel of your own, you need to commit yourself to the fact that this is going to be an ongoing learning process. As long as your vlog is running, you're going to be learning. The learning doesn't stop until you do. You're constantly going to be learning how to film better, how to vlog better, how to edit better, how to target your niche better - there's always something new to learn even if you're already an expert in your field.

- *Engaging with Audiences* - A big part of your vlogging success is going to depend on how you engage and interact with your audience. Without an audience, there would be no vlog for you to work towards turning it into a passive income stream. Audiences keep coming back to vloggers who are friendly and approachable and also someone who is responsive towards comments and feedback. Great vloggers are the ones who enjoy this sort of interaction with their viewers, and if this is something you enjoy too, you're going to enjoy your vlogging journey so much more.

Vlogging Earning Potential

Like blogs, this would depend on your content, viewership, the frequency with which you post, and how many views you're getting per video. Google pays vloggers approximately 68% for every $100 paid by an advertiser. The actual rate that an advertiser is going to pay you, however, would vary between $0.10 to $0.30 per view. The average usually hovers around $0.18 per viewing. This means that YouTubers, on average, can expect to earn approximately $18 for every 1,000 views on their video that they get, which works up to about $3-$5 per video view.

Of course, vloggers don't rely on just this alone for their passive income stream. Vlogging is just one of their many other revenue sources. Even on their vlogs, YouTubers who are pulling in a substantial amount annually are not doing it through ads or Google AdSense alone. Their income also comes from merchandise sales, as with famous YouTubers like Jeffree Star or Jake Paul for example, selling their own merchandise and products to their viewers. This contributes a lot of why they can earn as much as they do.

A lot of vloggers also supplement their earnings through sponsored content. Makeup vloggers, for example, agree to feature certain makeup products in exchange for payment. One finance vlogging channel, known as Minority Mindset, one shared in a video about how he earned $150,000 to help promote a product within the cryptocurrency niche. That's how lucrative sponsored content can be.

Debunking the Myths About YouTube and Vlogging
Don't let the myths and misconceptions hold you back from turning your vlogging channel into a potential passive income revenue. It's time to debunk the myths associated with vlogging so that you can get your channel underway:

- *Myth: You're Paid Based on Subscriber Numbers -* This one is a myth since subscriber counts have no bearings where Google AdSense is concerned.

The mechanics here are that YouTubers get paid for the amount of pre-roll ads that are viewed each time their video is seen. Which means that the more views a person gets on their video, the likelihood of people clicking on the ad content increases. From that perspective, subscriber numbers are imperative, but it does not mean that YouTubers get paid per subscriber.

- *Myth: YouTube Doesn't Allow Violent or Provocative Videos* - While YouTube's community guidelines talk about the kinds of content that should be posted, you can still find these videos available online. The guidelines exist, but the enforcement over such content isn't as strong as it should be. You should try to stay away from sharing this kind of content though, just to avoid any problems with your account being suspended or canceled later on. Sticking to videos that are within your niche and the subject your platform is based on is the best approach to take.
- *Myth: Shorter Videos Get More Viewership* - It's about quality content and not so much how long or short your videos are. Although your videos shouldn't be *too short* since it's unlikely you'll be able to deliver anything impacting or of quality if

your videos are only a couple of seconds long. At the same time though, you don't want to post video content that's *too long* either, since attention spans seem to get shorter and shorter as time goes by. What you do not want in your videos is content that is nothing more than just fluff. Unnecessary commenting or talking about irrelevant topics can also put you at risk of losing your audience's interest quickly.

Chapter 8. Create a Podcast

The podcasting world is rapidly growing because people are very fond of the idea of being able to listen to their favorite topics rather than having to read books or blogs on the subject. Podcasts can be listened to while people drive, clean, or even shower or get ready for their day—making them easily accessible to people with busy lives. For that reason, podcasts have grown exponentially in terms of their popularity in recent years and they can be a great passive income opportunity for people who want to generate profit from their activities.

Benefits of Hosting a Podcast

Hosting a podcast is not necessarily a stream of passive income because there is a consistent level of effort that needs to be applied in order for your platform to remain large enough to stay profitable. However, if you are willing to put the time in a podcast, it can generate income in many different ways, including several ones classified as passive income. If you want a unique opportunity to brand yourself and build a significant income by talking into a microphone for a few hours a week, podcasting is the way to go.

Podcasting is also beneficial because, if you run your own business, it can position you as an expert and have people turning to you for more information. The more you share your knowledge and expertise with your audience, the more they will come to trust you and the more likely they will be to turn to you and your business for support. As a result, you can massively improve both your reputation and your profits through a podcast.

How You Earn Money Through Podcasts

There are a variety of ways that you can earn money through a podcast but the two most popular ways include advertising for yourself and advertising for others. If you are advertising for yourself, you can earn money by promoting your products and services and increasing the amount of traffic crossing over your sales pages online. If you are marketing for others, you can charge for the amount of time you spend talking about and promoting their company, just like they do on traditional radio shows. Another way that you can get paid for advertising for other companies emulates affiliate marketing, whereby you will discuss a product and offer a unique checkout link or promo code for your audience. Each time someone pays for a product through your link or code you will be paid a compensation for their purchase.

Getting Started With Podcasting

Starting your podcast can be extremely simple, all you need is a topic to talk about, a platform to host you, and an audience to talk to. With these three ingredients, you can easily create a profitable podcast that will have you generating tons of profit in no time.

Selecting Your Niche

If you do not already have a niche, you are going to need to choose one to talk about on your podcast so that your audience knows why they should be listening to you. The most popular niches for podcasts these days fall under the business and self-help industries, which will likely be your best opportunities for selecting your specific sub-niche. From there, a great way to research your desired niche is to go to existing platforms like Podcasts on iOS and look at what the most popular stations are and how many views they are getting. You can also see how many other similar podcasts exist in the same sub-niches as these popular stations and how much traction they are getting. By taking a look at these sections and getting clear on what the best niches are, you can make sure that you are choosing one that is going to be popular enough for you to find viewers on.

After you have generated an idea of which niches are most popular, you need to think about what you are going to be most interested in learning about and talking about so that you can generate a higher viewership. If you talk about something you are uneducated in or that you are not passionate about, you will struggle to build a viewership because your audience will simply go elsewhere. People want to listen to someone who sounds passionate about what they are talking about and who shares credible and reliable information that is accurate on the given subject. They will not listen if your content lacks personality and passion or if you regularly promote misinformation or sound as though you have no idea what you are talking about.

Creating Your Podcast

After you have chosen a niche that will be popular and that will fit with your passions and knowledge, you need to actually create your podcast! Creating your podcast is the fun part, and it is also fairly easy because you do not have to do much in order to create it. You simply need a high-quality microphone, a focused subject for each episode, and a platform that you can post your podcast on.

Make sure that each episode has a clear subject and that you are offering a clear reason as to why you are talking about that information in particular. You should also try and leave your viewers with a lesson that has been fully engaged in, talked about, and wrapped up so that they have something to think about and consider in their own lives. By offering some form of wrap up, you also inspire your audience to begin thinking towards feasible solutions in their own lives so that they, too, can start learning their lessons and moving forward in their own lives. Ensure that each episode also includes your promotional content on it in a tasteful and direct manner so that you can earn your increased profits through your podcast!

Hosting platforms vary, but some great ones include BlogTalkRadio and iHeartRadio. These two platforms will allow you to host podcasts and will help share your podcast across many different hosting platforms, too. You can also manually submit your podcast proposal to several different popular podcast sites if you desire, though this will take far more time for you to achieve.

Promoting Your Podcast

If you host your podcast on platforms like BlogTalkRadio you will already have said platform promoting your podcast to a degree, anytime someone searches for content that is similar to yours. However, you will still need to promote your podcast in a more direct and complete manner if you want to amplify the number of viewers that you gain so that you can earn higher profits from your advertisements.

A great way of promoting podcasts is to have a well-rounded online platform that consists of a blog and a social media presence. Just a few high-quality targeted social media postings per week and a blog post per each podcast episode is plenty to start getting your marketing out there. For your blog, simply summarize your podcast and post a link to the episode so that your readers can find your latest episode and listen. For your social media, a few posts each week focused on the same subject that your blog is focused on will help you target your audience and capture their attention so that they are more likely to find your podcast. Through these two activities, you can massively amplify your number of viewers and increase your profits.

Note that podcasts may take time to develop a strong and reliable viewership, never mind one that trusts in you enough to actually purchase the products or services that you are promoting. However, if you stay consistent and continue to post new episodes on a regular schedule and you continue to market through social media and your blog, your viewership can grow massively in no time at all. As it does, your profitability will grow also and you will maximize the income that you can earn through this avenue.

If you want to further increase your profits, you can also leverage your social media presence for more profits through affiliate marketing and your blog for profits through advertising. By incorporating all three platforms into your profitable strategies, you can ensure that you are earning as much as possible making this income avenue even more effective and worthwhile in the long run.

Chapter 9. Online Courses

People love educating themselves, and online courses are an incredible way to do so. In the past 5 years, online courses have become more popular than ever before because they are short, self-lead, and can support people in learning a wealth of information about topics that actually interest them. Creating an online course does take some time up front, but once it is created, you can continue to sell that course for a long period of time—thus making it a highly passive form of income.

Benefits of Hosting Online Courses

The benefits of hosting online courses that are self-lead, which are sometimes called "evergreen courses," are broad. These courses are a great opportunity for you to position yourself as an expert, offer an ongoing income without having to put in any additional work, and cost almost nothing to make. Some people make a massive passive income online by producing a new course every month or every few months and posting it on a platform like Teachable or Udemy and they produce a great income through this. In some cases, people are earning over $100,000 a year just through creating and promoting their online courses.

If you wanted to, you could also host an online course that is done live—with you instructing said course through a platform like Skype or Facebook Live. In this particular circumstance, you could profit off of the live filming of the course by having paid members joining in on the process. Since the course is being held live, you can also charge more for tickets and earn a higher profit off of this first step. Then, you can go on to add the recordings to a course online and sell it to everyone else for slightly less than your live students paid. This way, you earn an even higher profit and the entire process was profitable.

How You Earn Money With Online Courses

Earning money online through courses is essentially the same as selling products online: every time someone purchases one of your courses you profit from that sale. You can easily continue selling as many digital downloads of your course as you desire and continue earning a profit for a long time. You may need to refresh your courses with some updated information or an updated look from time to time—otherwise, you have a great course online that can be sold for years to come.

Getting Started Making and Selling Online Courses

Creating and selling courses online is simple: you make your course, you post it on a hosting platform, and you market it to your desired audience.

Choosing Your Course Subject

Choosing what you want to teach about will ultimately depend on what your expertise is and what is marketable in the online space. A great way to get a sense of what people are looking for in online courses is to go to a platform like Udemy and browse their main pages. These pages will contain a significant amount of information regarding what is popular at the moment and what you will be most likely to earn a profit in. People are looking to online courses for many different types of information these days, from learning about how to design websites or develop video games to learning about how to meditate or how to market their business. You simply need to choose a subject to teach about and design your course!

Creating Your Course

Most online courses feature a variety of different learning tools to help people learn about the particular topic that is being taught on. Courses will regularly feature video content, written content, quizzes, and "homework" or workbooks for people to use as they go through the course. Although it may take longer, developing a few different types of content for your course will ensure that you have plenty to offer for your prospective students when they consider purchasing your course.

If you are particularly skilled in producing one or two types of content but not all of them, you can always outsource some of your content production to a skilled contractor. Again, Fiverr and Upwork are great resources for finding people who can generate workbooks, written content, or other materials for your course.

Choosing Your Hosting Platform

How you host your course will ultimately depend on how much time or effort you want to put into the hosting process. If you want it to be easy and done in a "plug it in and go" type manner, using Teachable or Udemy is your best option. Teachable will be the best option if you want a completely customized and self-branded website that reflects your business and does not show any signs of which hosting software you are using. However, it will cost you more per month in order to be able to use Teachable if you want to develop many courses and access features like instant payouts when people purchase your courses. Udemy is great if you want to have a platform that is plug in and go and if you do not necessarily care about branding your website personally. You can also partner with Udemy in terms of marketing by selecting an option whereby they earn a larger percentage from your sales but they also promote your course to their viewers. This means that you will show up higher on search listings and that you will be promoted across various platforms where Udemy has paid to sponsor posts or advertisements around the web.

If you want to have a more interactive and personalized platform, you might consider hiring a web developer to completely create your own website that is optimized for selling courses. This will cost you more, but if you are confident in your ability to turn a profit it can also give you far more features and be more flexible in terms of allowing you to do other things on your platform as well.

Promoting Your Online Course

After you have designed your course you simply need to promote it! The best way to promote online courses is to use services like Google Ads as this will help you get your course posted in many different areas across the internet. Facebook and Instagram also have great advertising platforms that can be used for you to promote your course to many other people. While you can leverage your social media presence to promote your course, it is not necessary if you do not already have one as most people will not attempt to search you up online when determining whether or not they want to take your course. Instead, they will look at the contents of the course and the pre-existing reviews of how other students have enjoyed the course and how they felt it was valuable in their learning experience.

Chapter 10. Peer-to-Peer Lending

With peer-to-peer lending you have an unlimited earning potential. This kind of business can be as big or as small as you like. It doesn't require a lot of time investment to get started, but you will need to do some research to find the right companies to invest in.

To get into this type of investment opportunity you'll have to go through one of the many online platforms that will help you to find a borrower to lend money too. Let's just take a look at some of them to see how they work.

Peer-to-peer lending is a relatively new method of financing where people can borrow money without the need of going through a financial institution to do so. This is all made possible through new technology and specialized peer-to-peer platforms that connect you the lender with the right borrower. You simply open an account and deposit your funds. The platform offers a variety of loan options and depending on how much you lend out, you will receive monthly payments in principle and interest for the duration of your loan.

- The Lending Club

This is the largest P2P lending platform in the world. As of now it has more than $20 billion of loans out. With the Lending Club, you can make small to medium sized loans that pay out over a fixed period of time that can range from as little as 36 months all the way up to 60 months. It plays the role of intermediary between the borrower and the lender. Once the loan has been funded, the borrower receives the money through a partner bank. It then sends the investor a note that serves as a security of payment.

- *Prosper*

Prosper only offers unsecured loans and never makes SME loans. The payback period is the same as with The Lending Club with loan amounts that can range from as small as $2,000 all the way up to $35,000. It uses the same notary business model as The Lending Club, but it also charges a closing fee to borrowers, which can range from 0.5% to 5%, depending on the loan type. You can invest with Prosper for as little as $25.

- *Upstart*

Upstart works a little differently from other peer-to-peer platforms. Both the Lending Club and Prosper charge the investor a small fee but Upstart generates all of its income from the borrower's fees. If the borrower defaults on his loan for some reason, Upstart gives the investor refunds using the origination fee it charged to the buyer when the loan was issued. This makes their platform much more appealing to investors however, there is a down side to it. As an investor you cannot personally choose which loans you will fund but instead, you'll select a specific grade to fund based on set criteria. You can invest in Upstart for as little as $100.

- *Kickstarter/Kickfurther*

Both of these platforms are considered to be public benefit corporations and are open for crowdfunding. With these sites, businesses and individuals can post details of their projects or expectations where individual investors can choose to support them or not.

With Kickstarter, the request for a loan is created by the individual or group behind a specific project. They set a funding goal and detail the timeline and expectations of their project. Kickstarter's role is simply as a means of connecting borrower and lender together and claims no responsibility for any project posted on their site. There is no screening process for any person or organization that posts on the site, and therefore no guarantee that those who post will use the funds as they detail in their requests.

In this type of posting, there is usually no monetary reward, but investors can receive rewards or gifts that hold a monetary value once the project is completed. Investors pledge a certain amount of money but do not need to pay it until the project reaches its funding goal. Therefore, in this type of platform it is strongly encouraged that you tread carefully to avoid losing your money to scams or other types of fraudulent claims.

Kickfurther works a little differently. It caters more to the businesses that are looking for funding to buy inventory. Each business must complete an application process and be approved and accepted before they can post on their site.

With Kickfurther, businesses are requesting that investors purchase their inventory and receive a consignment fee once the merchandise is sold. Again, you can pledge a certain dollar amount to contribute but do not need to pay until the business' funding goal is reached.

It is important to carefully study all the details of the offer including the payback terms, interest rate, and the time it is expected to see a return before you decide to invest. You can invest in either of these platforms with as little as $20.

What are the Risks?

In these types of ventures there is always risk. The obvious risk is that the borrower defaults on the loan and you lose your money. Another risk, in the case of Kickfurther, is that the business is unable to sell the inventory, tying up your money for an extended period of time. Always check to see if these platforms have a strategy to protect you from such losses before you decide.

Chapter 11. Google AdSense

Google AdSense is an ad network owned and operated by Google. As of today, it is the largest and highest paying ad network on the internet. Google AdSense is the program designed for website publishers who want to display targeted advertisements on their web pages and earn money when visitors view or click the ads.

Getting Started

To earn from Google AdSense, you will need to have a website or blog, although not all websites do well with AdSense. There are basically 2 key factors to consider if you want to make money with AdSense: you need great content and a lot of traffic.

There are also two types of website content: the one that attracts new visitors and the other that brings visitors returning daily. The ideal website for AdSense is one that is balanced for both. This ensures that just as you are attracting new visitors (traffic), you are also retaining loyal ones.

Examples of websites perfect for AdSense include but are not limited to: news blogs or websites, forums, niche sites, listicle blogs, how-to websites and online discussion boards. All you need is to find a layout that works well with displaying contents and AdSense ads.

It is important that you also understand the kinds of ads that AdSense will place on your website. Because advertisers have the options of creating ads in various formats (text-based, images, and/or video), you will need to create layouts that will accommodate the various formats, but ensure that they do not interfere with the content. The user always comes first.

Aside from display ads, AdSense offers another feature: custom search ads. This type of ad allows visitors to search for specific content on your website using AdSense. This is great because ads are displayed alongside the results of related searches.

Benefits of Google AdSense

There are various benefits of using Google AdSense aside from the fact that there are very few restrictions. It is easy to use, you get to earn consistent revenue from your websites and AdSense pays you on time.

How to make money for AdSense

To make money from AdSense, we have to first understand how AdSense calculates the earnings. We have to understand what CTR and CPC mean, what formula AdSense uses and how we can optimize the website or blog to get maximum benefits from AdSense.

CTR = Click Through Rate

This is the ratio of the number of users who click on an ad on a web page to the total number of visitors who visited the web page within a particular time frame. This is usually used to determine the effectiveness of advertisement on a website.

CPC = Cost Per Click

This is the amount earned by a website owner anytime a user clicks an advertisement on the web page. The earnings vary and it depends on the advertiser and niche, as some advertisers are willing to pay more than others.

The AdSense formula has 3 variables; Traffic, CTR and CPC.

The formula is recreated below.

Traffic x CTR x CPC = Revenue.

To ensure you continue to earn from AdSense, you have to find ways to increase any or all three of the variables. You can increase your CTR by placing your ads above the content. The higher your ads are, the greater the likelihood of increasing your CTR. You should also consider other factors like text color and size. You can increase your CPC by targeting high paying niches (Medical, Legal, etc.).

1.   Ad Placements

Where you place ads on your website determines how much you can benefit from Google AdSense. There are several locations on a web page where you can place ads for maximum visibility.

The header: this is above the content on the web page. It allows for maximum visibility and is most likely the ad with the highest CTR.

Between Paragraphs: This is also a great location for ads. Ensure you use a size of 300×250 for mobile and 728x90 for desktop.

Sidebar: Ads placed here also do pretty well. Use a 300x600 unit for both top and bottom sidebars.

Bottom of the content: Many website owners have reported great results from ads placed at the bottom of the content, especially when it was relevant to the content of their post.

2.   Increase Traffic

Traffic is the major determinant of how much you can make with AdSense. The more traffic you get, the greater the likelihood of a better CTR. Other tweaks to increasing revenue are available but the most stable way is through traffic. There are several ways you can increase traffic and they include:

Create great content. Give people something worth their time. You don't have to be a master at writing quality articles or creating a great post, just be good at what you are offering. Your content doesn't have to be long, but let it be real. There are great travel blogs raking in big money from AdSense; they just share their travel experience but also make it very interesting and educational. This converts to great traffic when users share and invite others to visit. Those people eventually become regular readers and invite others, which creates a chain reaction.

3.   Keywords

Using the right keywords in your content would help drive organic traffic to your website. It would be a shame if after investing in great content, proper ad placement and all the necessary tweaks; you fail at attracting organic traffic due to a lack of appropriate keywords. Research keywords that are suitable for your content, find their ranks, and also check Google Trends to get an idea of popular keywords.

4.   Map out an Efficient Strategy

It is ideal that you have an original strategy that works for you. This helps you to keep focus on what you're interested in and what direction you want your business to go. There a couple of strategies you can adopt.

You can choose to create lots of content with string keywords that help you generate organic search traffic, or you can choose to focus on filling little pieces of content with "monster keywords". Whatever you are comfortable with and what works for you would be fine. In my opinion, creating great content with string keywords is usually the best approach. Aside from the value it creates for your users or visitors, you are likely to have repeat visits more often than from content with "monster keywords".

5.   AdSense is Not the Only Ad network

Ad networks such as Media.net and Alpha are gradually carving their own place in the ad network ecosystem. Diversifying your ad network also helps in case there are problems with AdSense or if you are banned. That way, you won't lose all of your money. Sometimes, you will find that these other ad networks are actually outperforming AdSense.

6.   Explore Other Offers

Do not get stuck working your website or blog to serve only AdSense. This practice of incorporating other online products and businesses is a good way to diversify and take great advantage of your platform. Do not aggressively pursue affiliate marketing to avoid the AdSense hammer but try still to diversify. Create content that promotes affiliate links but don't overdo it.

Mistakes to Avoid

There are a few mistakes to avoid when designing your layout to allow for AdSense. Avoid placing ads adjacent to images, next page buttons and in any way that would attract accidental clicks on your web page. This will cause you to avoid a penalty called the Nessie penalty.

The Nessie penalty is imposed by AdSense when you have an unusually high CTR. These accidental clicks can sometimes arise as a result of your layout or in some cases from your aggressive marketing. In all, it is advised that you try to keep your CTR as moderate as possible.

AdSense is a viable way to make serious money online with a website. The key is to building traffic and implementing the measures we have highlighted here. You are also required to regularly update your knowledge and implement a lot of new strategies to find out what works best for you. There is a lot of trial and error in any business, so do not become apprehensive if something fails at first. Keep trying and improving your strategy and it will eventually work out.

Chapter 12. Real Estate

Investing in real estate is one of the best ways to make passive income, but it does require you to make some upfront investment. Please be aware that this chapter will be a lot more "theoretical" and with a lot more bullet points as compared to others—so read it a couple of times to really get its essence.

Investing in real estate has some great benefits! You can really make some excellent side income out of it.

How Does Real Estate Investment Work?

To make money in real estate, one thing you have to remember is to have a positive cash flow, meaning at the end of the month you should have made more money compared to what you spent on it.

The question is: Should you sell or rent out? Rent it out. As long as you hold on to the property, the value will go up, so it is always recommended to rent it out rather than selling it.

In order to make money off real estate you will have to buy a property, and regardless of what property it is, you will have to invest a lump-sum of cash. For most of the people, this would mean getting a mortgage. This would equate to a long-term commitment. Once you decide to rent out your property, you will have to use the income generated by the rent to cover all your in-house expenses like repairs etc. If you have the funds, buy cash so you can start making some serious profits from the beginning rather than waiting 15 to 20 years.

Investing in Real Estate

I can understand how everyone won't have the lump-sum money to spend on a property. There are a few ways to secure a property rental if you look hard enough:

Sell assets you do have like your car, jewelry or stocks and bonds.

Find an investment partner.

Get a loan privately.

Take out a mortgage.

Take over the mortgage payments of someone who is in financial distress and cannot afford it themselves.

The Financial Costs

If you can't find the full amount, then it is highly recommended that you pay as much as you can as a down payment. This can lower the monthly repayments you will be responsible for. Also, on taking a mortgage, you should be prepared to cover the costs for a few months while waiting for a tenant.

The rent you will be asking for your new property will depend on a lot of factors. Depending on the size of the house and neighborhood, it can vary.

Deciding the rate of your renting.

The rent you ask for is the most critical determinant in your real estate investment endeavors. So how do you go about setting a rent rate that will provide you with the best returns and be attractive to potential tenants?

The first thing to do is to find reasonably-priced real estate you can afford. It is also advised, to keep in mind that you should not invest in a rental property if the purchase price is twelve times more than what you expect to receive in rent for a year.

Factors to Consider When Calculating Rent

First of all, do some research and find out the average rent in your area. Deduct related essential expenses such as mortgage repayments, real estate taxes and insurance costs (remember to divide each of these cost factors by 12) and maintenance and repairs fees (set aside a healthy allowance for these costs).

In the beginning, asking for too high of a rent rate may lead you not to find a suitable tenant easily, and your rental sits empty for a few months. At the same time, you need to make sure you don't underestimate what maintenance will cost you, and you end up paying more than you budgeted for.

Your maintenance and repairs costs will depend on how old your property is, who your tenants are and how well they look after it so, for example, a house with young students may require more regarding cosmetic repair than a home with more mature tenants. The third consideration is whether maintenance will be D-I-Y or outsourced to a contractor or handled via a real estate management agency for a monthly management fee.

D-I-Y repairs mean lowered costs but the inconvenience of being available 24/7 should an emergency arise.

Finding the right balance between a fair market-related rate and a good value tenant and you have found the perfect formula for consistent and favorable returns on your real estate rental investment for the long term.

Do Your Research.

You will need to conduct a thorough real estate search before you purchase your first buy-to-let property. In your search, you will need to base your choice on a number of factors. A good piece of advice is to look very carefully at the location, even if the property seems a bit run down but the area is excellent, it promises greater returns over the long term, and if you have some more money to invest in the future fix it up it will only lead you to make more money.

Slowly Build Up.

Managing more than one piece of property can be overwhelming for anyone regardless it is an experienced landlord or not. Starting off with rental real estate requires a learning curve, slowly invest and it shall grow. If you want to, you can start by renting out your basement or room. Slowly build up from there.

Property Types to Invest In

As you become a real estate investor, there are choices of property types to choose from. All of them have advantages and disadvantages to each, so picking them based on your need is imperative.

There are some types of real estate that are more ideal for beginner property investors to get their feet wet, so to speak. Here are a few suggestions on what kind of property that offers favorable advantages.

Single-Family Homes

This is the most comfortable property to find tenants for. Many new families or couples choose single-family homes as their preferred choice for long-term rentals. This type of real estate investment makes it an ideal opportunity for a beginner investor as they offer better tenant quality value, which means more financially stable, more likely to look after the property and pay rent regularly. The single-family home is a detached or a semi-detached property unit with a yard or driveway as a distinct dividing line from neighboring properties.

Advantages:

Investing in the property can greatly increase the price you bought it for.

Provides greater returns on investment over the long-term.

Provided it is located in a growing neighborhood with great family people, and it was well maintained the property would grow its resale value.

Property taxes will be lower as compared to multi-family units and commercial real estate.

Management costs are lower if your tenants are great tenants.

Disadvantages:

Cash flow is dependent on one, unlike multi-family units. If a tenant moves out and you have to wait a while for another, the empty house could cause you to pay for the mortgage for the times it is left without a tenant.

Multi-Family House

This type of real estate can be comprised of duplexes, triplexes, or quadplexes on a single plot. A housing can be accommodated for two to four families. Each unit provides a rental opportunity. This type of real estate is easier to maintain and manage as compared to having more than one single family units to look after.

Advantages:

More financing options available for the investor.

If one tenant leaves, cash flow is still generated from the tenants of the other units.

If you, the owner, lives in one of the units, you can benefit from the owner-occupied mortgage rate.

Disadvantages:

The tenant pool for multi-family rentals is smaller, so there are few buyers when you do decide to resell.

Buying multi-family units are relatively more expensive than single family homes.

Repairs may affect more than unit especially if flooding is the cause.

Condominium

A condo is a single unit in a larger building. The best advantage to opting to invest in condos is their low maintenance factor. In addition to this, the exterior of the house or building will be taken care of. All you have to take care of is interior of the house

Other advantages:

Amazing recreational things to do such as swimming, gym, etc.

Disadvantages:

Will be sharing your living space with a lot of people

Privacy is limited.

Tips for Beginner Investors in Rental Real Estate

Here is some excellent advice for people considering this as their stream of passive income:

1.   Look at real estate rentals as a long-term investment. This will provide you with higher returns on your investment.

2.   Start with a ready-to-move-in property. Places that need work are ideal for those with some experience in property investment. Renovations usually take longer than expected and cost more than anticipated.

3.   *When it comes to negotiating and purchasing, seek the experience of a professional real estate agent. He or she will guide you in the right direction.*

4.   Conduct your research on the property market before your first purchase. Read up on trends, how to manage property rentals, etc.

5.   Consider being an owner-occupant as it comes with lesser responsibilities of being a landlord.

6.   Make sure your credit score is good before looking at getting a loan.

7.   *Investigate all your financing options before pulling the trigger, like hard money loans and real estate syndication.*

8.   Start to network with contractors, suppliers, realtors and other investors and landlords. They might be of great help in the future.

It is recommended to be business-minded and to approach real estate investing like you are running a business. Take a business course if necessary to learn about the financial terminology, accounting and financial statements and principles of building wealth.

Do have an exit strategy in mind. You don't want to focus on your real estate investment plan failing but as the future is inevitable for no one, having a plan B will help minimize potential loss. Ideally selling your property will help you with that.

How Much Money Can You Make?

To be honest, this really depends on how much money you have invested and how many properties you have rented out. But an average is $50,000 a year, now you can probably make more than that, but it requires you to have more properties. But the best part about this method is that you will have sellable investments, meaning you will most likely not lose money, simply sell it.

In all your excitement you may be tempted to head out and look for the first available property that looks profitable and sit back and wait for the rental income to come in. The reality of real estate investment is that it takes time for things to fall into place. It takes time to find the right property and to make it yours to rent then finally. Also, there are a lot of rules and legal matters to go through before you get started on this. The best way to avoid making mistakes is to be aware of what they can be and to not exercise them. Connect with other landlords. Their knowledge and experience can be used to better your chances of not facing any adversities in your real estate investments.

Chapter 13. Making Passive Income as An Artist/Creative

The reason I chose to put artists in a separate group is that there is too much stigma facing the art industry. By art, I don't necessarily mean drawing or painting but any art form that people think one cannot make a career out of. For me, artists are those that make and sell candles, underground musicians, if you make shoes, guitars, jam, chili and so many more. They use their imaginations to make things that we need on a day to day basis. They may not have enough money to advertise, but they still want to make a living from their ideas. This chapter is meant for anyone that uses their imagination to make anything.

How to Earn a Living as An Artist or Creative

1.   Stock Photography

Some people don't know that you can sell your photographs online to people. They assume that you can only get money by getting clients to pay for your skills. There are many people out there that take photos of buildings, plants, animals or landscapes that are not paid by someone to do so. They enjoy the work and would like to know how they can make more money from their photos. There are websites online that buy photographs from talented photographers. Depending on the site, the photographer can be offered a commission every time someone pays to use the photo, or the website can just give the photographer a one-time fee, and they now own the photo. If you have those beautiful pictures f your phone or DSLR camera and don't know what to do with them, you can create a portfolio and approach one of these websites, e.g., Shutterstock. Other sites include Alamy, Picfair, EyeEm, Foap, iStockphoto, Dreamstime, Free digital photo Getty Images, etc. Even if you get a commission from the website, you have no control over what the person who is licensed by the website does with it. Paying you a commission is the better deal as you will be receiving online payments as long as people use your work. How can you have your work approved by one of these websites?

Have a theme for each photo you take and choose the best from each theme. They only need the best shot;

otherwise they could reject your work because of duplication. Keep your submission to 10 photos.

Some websites have millions of photographs, and they have different categories for each one of them. It is already hard to get in one of these websites, but it is even harder if you submit a photo in a popular category. Do something unique that they may not have seen before, and you are guaranteed to be accepted. Keep your best materials for later and start with a simple yet beautiful shot.

Avoid submitting photos that capture brand names or trademarked items. That would cause your photo to be rejected for copyright infringement. Avoid people's faces, public places or commercial objects. You may submit them in the future if you're accepted.

Keep your images the recommended size. Ensure that they are visible and meet the standards of the website you are submitting to.

Edit your photo before submitting. Many software allows you to do so. You can remove vignettes, add color among other things. Never submit photos with lens flares.

2.   Licensing your art to third parties

Here, you have to look for people who need your art say a photograph, music, application and sell them a license to use your product for your work. You will earn more money this way as you are the one that gets to set a price for what you think your work is worth. You will need to have a unique product and look for people that you think can buy a license for it. There are many ways to do that, i.e., through social media, email lists and sending out proposals. Don't just wait for people to stumble upon your work. You can market your work anywhere on the internet where you can reach more people faster. You get to make money licensing the product every time they renew the license while you still get to keep your product.

3.   eBooks

We have talked about self-publishing and selling eBooks before in this book; therefore I shall skip through this. Although I should remind you that the book should be based on what you are doing. You can do an introduction of what you so and then be creative with your content. You can make an instruction guide or any other information you may have to share with your reader.

4.   Start a Blog Related to your Art

Any business out there is required to have a website in this day and age, so should you for your art. For people to take you seriously, they need to see your portfolio or sample of what you can do before they are convinced to buy. Having a blog also allows you to apply other passive income generating avenues such as advertising, affiliate marketing, email marketing and selling your art online. You can also create a membership site that you can share with your paying audience special work and your process. You make a monthly income as opposed to making them buy something just once. You will require to do more work of creating new products to keep the members satisfied, and you will need more sophisticated software to maintain your site to manage payments and ease of use by users. Despite the workload, you will definitely earn more this way than all the other methods.

5.   Make Money by Selling Social Media Shout-outs to other Smaller Artists

If you have a good following on social media, you can make money by approaching smaller talented artists and ask them if they would pay for a shout out. Some will agree, and some may not have the money to pay you so it's up to you if you can help out someone talented by using your platform for good. It is important to remember that you should only be giving shout-outs to people in your niche. You don't want to confuse your audience by introducing a different niche in your space unless it's a collaboration that is tied somehow to your niche.

6.   Be a Part of an Artist Collective

It is always better to share ideas with fellow artists than going about it alone. Most people feel the need to try and make it on their own when it can be easier as a group. Artistry, for example, is one of those industries that wouldn't work properly if people failed to communicate and inspire each other. Rather than struggle as a starving artist, link up with other artists that can help you sell your product or art. With people doing similar things or even different things but in the artistic industry, you can come up with cool projects you can do together. You can start art galleries, and you can make niche groups or clubs. You and a group of your similar minded friends can look for ways you can benefit the community you live in through youth projects, teaching classes to the needy and help inspire more people to join the arts.

How to Make an Online Course and Make Money Selling It

The reason I have not included this topic of creating and selling your own online course as a way to make a passive income as an artist is that it is the main way for an artist to make money. The only thing an artist really has is the talent and what better way to leverage that talent than to package it and sell it online. Multiple platforms allow an artist to do that but before then let's look at how to create an online course.

1.   Find a Subject Matter

You already identified the skill that you have and want to share with the world. Its time to look at it in-depth and see if you have enough material to fit an entire course. You will have to come with some interesting materials that people would be interested in paying you for. Create a title that includes the core skills your course will impart on your students. In your description ad two or three more core skills that you promise they will leave with after they complete your course. These are what will enable you to plan your lessons, make marketing easier and deliver your point across to your students.

2.   Find Out if there is a Need

This is important because if people are not interested in the topic you want to teach, then there is no need to do it at all. This is where you can look at what people are saying online and find what else you can include in your course. You need to start learning more about our course so that you are not caught unaware when questions start coming in.

3.   Make a Teaching Plan and Course Outline

You have to consider your time and when you are available for the lessons. Talk to your community online and ask them when they are free to take your course and plan around that. You then have to think of how to structure your lessons. Are they in modules or weeks? What should each module contain and how can I make it as interactive as possible? How long are each module and the course in general? Make sure you cover all the bases before you dive in.

4.   Consider your Teaching Methods.

Each student is different, and you might want to cater to their different learning styles. Some learn from looking at pictures while others like working on the lessons through a quiz at the end. You can look for feedback to find the best delivery method like text, video, guides, audio, worksheets, etc. You can combine two methods to teach your course.

5.   Make your Content

This s where the bulk of your work will be. You have to ensure that you deliver something useful to the people who will take your course; otherwise, you will receive a tone of bad reviews. You also have to make the workload easy for them to follow and ask questions when they don't. The videos and audio should be clear for everyone to follow what you are saying. Brand your material attractively so that people know what they are taking. After you finish the work, go through it again and make sure it is good enough for the students. Before you get cocky and think that you have created the best course ever, it's important to remember that everything you have written can be found free on the internet. Packaging your work in a convenient, easy to understand way is what makes people interested in your course. They want to know everything related to your core skills without having to consult other sources.

Here is how to sell your course online:

1. Plan How to Sell the Course

Assuming you already have a website, add the features that you will need to deliver the course to your community. If you don't, start with that. There are multiple plugins especially on WordPress that help you with the selling and delivery of an online course. If you are not skilled in making such a website, you can sell your course on other websites that already offer that service such as Skillshare or Udemy. You will, however, have to share with the website a part of your earnings depending on the sales you make. The advantages of these websites are that you don't have to worry about delivery systems as they take care of selling the course and processing payments. You will have to reduce the cost of your course because the competition can get very steep. You also don't control your work because you are not running the course. There is a better option that combines two of the different delivery styles. You get to control what the content looks like but still maintain the benefits of an online course website. Examples of such websites include Ruzuku and Teachable.

2.   Upload your Course Online

Depending on the platform you choose to deliver your course, you will need to customize your course to look appealing to the students. You will have to use visible fonts, an attractive color scheme and your logo for branding purposes. People need to be able to recognize your brand.

3.   Marketing

As with everything else in this book, people need to know what you are doing before they come on board. You will need to use multiple social media sites, blog, email list and many other avenues to tell people why they need to take your course. Social media has paid pay-per-click advertising options that you can pay for to reach more people in your niche. It also allows you to see who is interested in our page among other insights that can help you put together a marketing plan that suits everyone on your community. In your marketing pitches, focus more on what the students will get out of the course rather than focusing on selling the course itself. You can tell them what to expect if they take the course. If you have other courses, offer them testimonials that can be verified so that they can believe you. You need to market your work in your community because they already trust you. Selling to strangers is harder because they don't know you and cannot substantiate if you are genuine or not.

4.   Update your Course Often

Things change every day and so is what is in your course. You need to do frequent research to improve your content, adding what you think people may want to know and removing what is already obsolete. Keep going through the links in your course to see if they are still working. You never know if the website you were referring to remove the content or stopped existing altogether. These small details are what separates you from bad reviews.

5.   Collect Feedback

If you are a genuine seller, you will want to follow up with your students to see if they got anything from your work. If they had any problems, it's important to know so that you can solve them in the future. Take their experiences so that you can use them for your testimonials in the future.

6.   You can Create more Content Through the Steps Outlined Above

Chapter 14. How To Leverage Social Media For Passive income

Anybody can profit on the off chance that they're willing to place in more hours at work, yet not every person has opportunity to do it. That is the place automated revenue proves to be useful.

Profiting while you rest (truly) feels extraordinary, but at the same time it's shrewd. On the off chance that you can procure a check without a ton of work, you've set yourself up for an agreeable future. Luckily, the web is basically intended to create easy revenue — it just requires a little information and exertion.

1) Use Your Blog

In the event that you haven't just made an adapted blog, at that point start one today. It's perhaps the most ideal ways you can produce pay without a great deal of work. The extraordinary thing about a blog is that it regularly takes under 10 hours of the week to keep up, yet it can possibly make a similar income as a 40-hour work week.

Simply beginning a blog isn't sufficient to create easy revenue, however. You'll have to set up activities that will keep on working when you're nowhere to be found. Here are probably the most well known techniques:

Compose an eBook: After you've composed a few blog entries on a specific subject, it's genuinely simple to incorporate the data into an eBook, which you can sell on the web. In case you're just selling each duplicate for $0.99, and you sell 1K duplicates in a month, that is an extra $1K in your pocket.

Promote: Advertisements are the most well-known type of automated revenue for websites. Organizations will pay as much as possible to promote on your blog in the event that it gets enough traffic.

Compose Affiliate Reviews: With an offshoot connection implanted into your audit, you'll profit each time somebody taps on a connection as well as buys an item.

Accomplice Up: Another type of subsidiary connecting comes when you join forces with another organization; you can offer a coupon code for an item or administration sold on another blog. Each time somebody utilizes that coupon code, you'll get paid.

2) Make Videos

Recordings are very well known via web-based networking media today, especially now that Facebook has organized the autopay highlight. At the point when a video starts playing, most of shoppers won't click away. They'll watch the video completely.

Thus, on the off chance that you can make an extraordinary video and market it to general society, you can gain huge cash from ads. At the point when on the finance stage, YouTube will pay a couple of pennies each time somebody watches the video, which are reserves that originated from different promoters. A couple of pennies isn't much in the event that you just get a couple of hundred perspectives, however on the off chance that you get many thousands and that's just the beginning, you can make a pretty penny.

Viral recordings are likewise extraordinary for creating automated revenue. When the video is made, it will circle the web through online life and YouTube. You can profit from commercials and perspectives for a considerable length of time after a viral video courses the web.

3) Social Media Management

This doesn't remove much from your day by day timetable, and you can make a considerable amount of cash from your endeavors. Regardless of whether you're dealing with your very own social profile or assuming control over the administration for a business, there are tricky ways you can assemble some additional salary as an afterthought.

The initial step is to construct a decent after. At that point, you can share substance and connects and create a discourse about each. Organizations will pay you to share this substance on the off chance that you get enough commitment.

You can likewise interface your site to web-based life on the off chance that you have items or administrations worth selling. On the off chance that shoppers appreciate the substance you share, they'll tail you back to your site, and you can take advantage of this association.

Chapter 15. What to Avoid

As with everything else out there, there is a good side and a bad side when it comes to making a passive income. You need to avoid those ever so popular money making schemes that so many people are falling into. Keep in mind that there are people who promise that you will start off small and end up on top of the world with money rolling into your bank account. Sure, they may be doing great, but this isn't a guarantee that you're going to be just like them.

Passive Income Sites that Guarantee the Moon:

There are passive income sites out there that will promise you the moon, but you must consider the time you need to put into it. Actually, when looking up the definition of passive income, we find that a passive income is money you make while not doing anything at all. Passive income sites will have you believing that you can set up a website, let people know what you're selling, and sit back and watch the money roll in. This is far from the truth, because if you don't work on getting traffic to your site, money isn't going to roll in.

Before you sit back and relax, you have to do the work and it is much more than just setting up a site.

Paying Money to Make Money:

If a site asks you to pay money in order to make money, it's probably bad news. An example of this is those binary option sites that ask for a huge deposit before even trying it... Before you do something like this, do your research and see what others have to say about the company. After all, you're here to make money, not spend money to learn how to make money.

Giving Out Your Bank Account Information:

For some reason, people can't just use the world banking system – they need access to that personal bank account in order to issue payment to you. Unfortunately, most times, with this, the only direction the money goes is out of that account and into their account where you won't be able to recover it. So take it from me, don't ever give our your personal bank account information online.

Chapter 16. Tips on Succeeding

Some people will tell you that making a passive income online isn't going to work, but they don't know what they're talking about. Just because they've had a bad experience with it, or because they've never done it before, they think it's not possible. However, I am living proof that it is possible to make a passive income – here's some tips on succeeding ...

Be Easy to Find:

You must be easy to find. There are a couple of places that your product/service needs to be found. To start with, you need visibility on Yahoo, Bing, and of course, Google. By doing a little bit of SEO and keyword research, it's possible to get your site to show up at the top of the list. You can use the content on your website in order to get to the top of the list. Mind you, you shouldn't have to put money towards getting a top ranking, but if you want, you can. The idea here, however, is to create as much profit, with as little overhead costs as possible and a PPC, in my opinion, is overhead.

Make it Easy to Find Your Product:

When someone visits your site, they don't want to have to dig for the products/services you're offering. Don't create a maze that people have to crawl through. Try to capture attention, put it in big bold font.

Know What You're Talking About:

If you despise sports, don't go into the sports niche - if you despise video games, don't go into the video game niche. Go into a niche that you know about. What are you good at? What do you like doing? If you find video games boring, this will shine through in your writing and you won't be able to properly interact in the comment section or on social media if you don't know what you're talking about. If you appear to know what you're talking about, people will be more willing to pay money for your ebooks/services.

A Simple Checkout Process:

When I come across a complicated checkout process, I hit the exit button. Your checkout process needs to be as simple and secure as it can be. If it could be one button, that would be perfect. Many sales are lost due to payment systems being poorly constructed.

Join Master Mind Groups:

Go on Facebook and find mastermind groups that you're interested in. If you're interested in dropshipping then join a group that talks about it. You'll learn much faster because you're around others who know the ropes already and can give you some guidelines to what you're doing wrong and how to improve it.

Invest in a Mentor:

A mentor isn't cheap, I'm not going to lie. My mentor costed me $400 an hour however it was well worth it. He showed me what I was doing wrong etc. It's a steep investment but if you keep what they said in mind, you'll succeed. Eventually you'll get to a personal level where you can get the advice for free and even merge businesses etc. You'll be saving much more money with having a mentor by learning from their mistakes and also shortcut your success by avoiding what they did.

Don't be a Fu*king Dabbler:

If you're going to get this work, you need to commit. People think writing 3 blog posts a month will take you to 6 figures. No. Just no. Commit your ass. You need to write at least one blog post every 2 days at the minimum, no less. If you're going to do dropshipping, if you don't make 10k in your first month then don't quit. Getting rich quick is very much possible, that's why there's so many young millionaires nowadays but getting rich overnight isn't possible. Don't dabble in one pool and give up, you have to commit.

Have More than One Stream of Income:

The problem with most people nowadays is that they have a job and that's all their income. If they get fired or the company goes bust, they're homeless. It's the same as online, Amazon can suddenly go bust. You need more than 1 stream of income. It's been statistically proven that millionaires have at least 7 income streams so if you've got at least 3, you should be alright if one goes down the drain. I personally have 10, I'm close to being a millionaire (not one yet) but I would be having well more than 20 if Google didn't change their algorithms and policies didn't always change, but hey that's life! With the time of the other passive income streams you should always try to make more passive income, whether that'd be physical or online streams.

Conclusion

Based on the new economy, merged with the Internet, we have numerous ways to earn an income. Passive income is a great way to earn extra money to pay our bills, make ends meet, and even fund our travels with little input on our end. You also don't need to quit your day job to do so because most passive income stream explained in this book is ideal to be conducted on an online basis.

What's even better is that you can use whatever skills you already pose to kick-start a passive income stream or use the many different platforms that enable you to make money such as through self-publishing, affiliate marketing, and even Cashback rewards.

Although the premise of passive income is to contribute as little effort as possible to bring in your income, you still need to exert your time and a considerable amount of work to build up the foundations, so that you can reap your passive income later.

The business ideas listed in this book enable you to start generating passive income fairly quickly, but take note that none are get-rich-quick schemes.

With time, effort, and maybe a little bit of monetary investment, your passive income business will earn you a pretty good amount of money over time.